WRITE THROUGH IT: PARENT EDITION

a guided journal

paint the town
PEDIATRICS

Write Through It: A Guided Journal for Parents of Tweens & Teens

Published by Paint the Town Pediatrics

Get Your Free Companion Gift

Go to www.writethroughitbonus.com to receive 30 Days of self-care secrets, conversation starters, and positive affirmations.

Check Out Our Other Listings

Write Through It: A Guided Journal For Teen Girls

Color Through It: Anxiety and Stress Relieving Coloring Book for Tween and Teen Girls

This Journal Belongs To:

INTRODUCTION

"What's with the attitude and moodiness and how long will this last?"

"How can I make sure my child is not sad or depressed?"

"How can I get my child to open up?"

All these thoughts run through your head as you bring your child to my office. My nurse checks your child's height and weight, we talk about the vision screening and medication refills, and then the conversation shifts.

I break the silence and I see you repositioning in your seat. Your child gives an uncomfortable laugh as we start to talk about more serious topics...puberty, relationships, drugs, alcohol, sex, and mental health.

I see the tears in your eyes as your child admits that they're sad and depressed more often than not. I feel your pain as you learn that your child feels like they're not good enough.

I think about all of the conversations that don't quite go this way. The conversations where the kids remain silent or the parent reacts in a manner that pushes the child even further away.

I know there's so much more to be said.

The conversations can be difficult. As tweens and teens navigate their transition to adulthood, they often seek more privacy and independence, and therefore become more silent because to them, "parents just don't understand." Their peer relationships become increasingly significant, their hormones thrust them onto an emotional rollercoaster, and often they are overwhelmed by their feelings and struggle to express themselves.

I know you feel helpless sometimes. I know you don't always know how to get through to your child. I know you wonder when did your talkative kid become a silent tween/teen. I know you want to protect your child but don't even know how at times. As a mom and pediatrician, I understand that sometimes, you just may not know what to do.

But together, here, we can bridge the gap. This journal was designed not only to give you a safe place to vent your parenting frustrations. It's chock full of tools and prompts to help you manage emotions and improve communication and connection with your tween/teen.

Here's how you can get the most out of this guided journal.

MONTHLY INTENTIONS

If you want to thrive, not just survive, as you navigate the tween and teen years, setting monthly intentions can be a powerful tool to enhance your parenting journey. Kick off your month with my **Parent Prescriptions**, where I share an encouraging letter with you to motivate you and reassure you that you've got this! You'll then be given creative space to reflect and set your specific and achievable intentions that align with your goals for building a deeper connection with your child for the month. Intentions are simply desires and thoughts so don't stress. Just focus more on how you want to feel versus what you want to achieve when setting your intentions and you're all set.

Setting monthly intentions allows you to be intentional in your approach to parenting, ensuring that you are nurturing your relationship with your child in a way that is both meaningful and fulfilling.

Remember, monthly intentions are not about perfection but about progress. They provide you with a roadmap for exploring new avenues of communication, understanding, and love. Embrace the flexibility to adjust your intentions as needed and to celebrate every step forward, no matter how small.

WEEKLY CHECK-UPS

Change doesn't happen overnight, but when you take the time to set goals, show gratitude, and set weekly intentions, it's as easy as 3-2-1! Reflect on what matters to you with a journaling prompt, focus on a weekly intention, or simply vent your frustrations on the pages.

You'll find my **Communication Builders**, where I share quick and easy ways to boost the communication with your tween/teen. Try them out and write about how these communication builders changed the dynamic with you and your child.

Look out for my **Stress Busters** too. Use the space to vent your frustrations and use the stress boosting exercises and activities to manage parental stress and maintain emotional well-being.

I'll also pop in with **Positivity Bolsters**, key quotes to keep you motivated and encouraged along the way. Use this space to write about the positive things about your parenting, your children, your communication, your wins, etc...

Lastly, take your relationship with your tween/teen to the next level with **Bond Boosters**. Spending quality time with each other and learning more about each other is how you grow. You can keep track of all of the wonderful memories you create here.

NOTE-TO-SELF

Use this space for when you need to get things on your heart and mind out and onto paper. Use these blank pages to write out notes, scribble down reminders, doodle to-do lists, or whatever you need.

Parenting tweens and teens is not always easy but if you can write through it, you can get through it. I encourage you to use this space as your sanctuary for self-discovery and parenting growth.

As you begin your journaling journey, may you find the strength to navigate the challenges with grace, the patience to celebrate the joys, and the openness to cherish the unique bond that blossoms between you and your child.

I'm cheering you on, one word at a time! Happy Writing!

Love,

Charnetta Colton-Poole, M.D.

aka Dr. CeCe

Rx PARENT PRESCRIPTION

Directions:

Dear Parent,

Embrace the journey of parenting a tween/teen, knowing that challenges bring learning and growth.

Signature Dr. Charnetta

Date Today

Let's Be Intentional!

Now's the time to think about your desires for the month. Reflect on the parenting prescription and write how it makes you feel.

Now, take a moment to jot down your deepest desires you'd like to achieve this month (e.g. - spend more time with my kids, feel better in my own skin, etc...). Reflect on them often.

THIS WEEK

Dates

3 Goals I'd Like To Achieve This Week:

1

2

3

2 Things I Am Grateful For:

1

2

My Intention For This Week:

Mark the day(s) you achieved this intention. Write notes about how it feels to complete it.

M	T	W	T	F	S	S

This week, I intend to initiate 2 meaningful conversations with my tween/teen to better understand their thoughts and feelings.

Describe a typical day in your life as a parent of a tween/teen. What emotions do you experience throughout the day, and how can you bring more balance to your routine?

COMMUNICATION BUILDER

Active Listening: Practice focused listening without interrupting to understand your child's perspective completely.

THIS WEEK

____
Dates

3 Goals I'd Like To Achieve This Week:

1.

2.

3.

2 Things I Am Grateful For:

1.

2.

My Intention For This Week:

Mark the day(s) you achieved this intention. Write notes about how it feels to complete it.

M	T	W	T	F	S	S

This week, I will acknowledge any past mistakes and use them as opportunities to grow and improve our interactions.

How do you help your tween/teen navigate peer pressure and make choices aligned with their values? How can you help them set boundaries?

"In the chaos of the tween and teen years, remember that love is the steady anchor your child needs."

THIS WEEK

Dates

3 Goals I'd Like To Achieve This Week:

1

2

3

2 Things I Am Grateful For:

1

2

My Intention For This Week:

Mark the day(s) you achieved this intention. Write notes about how it feels to complete it.

M	T	W	T	F	S	S

My intention is to address conflicts calmly and constructively, teaching my tween/teen healthy ways to resolve disagreements.

Reflect on the values you wish to instill in your tween/teen. How can you model these values through your actions and words?

STRESS BUSTER

When faced with a challenge, take a deep breath and give yourself a moment to collect your thoughts before responding. Now, write or draw whatever is on your mind or heart.

THIS WEEK

____
Dates

3 Goals I'd Like To Achieve This Week:

1.

2.

3.

2 Things I Am Grateful For:

1.

2.

My Intention For This Week:

Mark the day(s) you achieved this intention. Write notes about how it feels to complete it.

M	T	W	T	F	S	S

I will set aside dedicated quality time to engage in 1-2 activities that my child enjoys, creating a stronger bond.

Describe a time when your tween/teen made a mistake. How can you use this as a teaching moment and support them through the learning process?

Bond Booster

Game Night: Play board games, card games, or video games together, adding a touch of friendly competition and laughter.

Rx

Parent Prescription

Directions:

Dear Parent,

Sometimes your child will make you want to scream. Instead of screaming at them during challenging moments, take a moment to express your feelings on paper so you can approach them with compassion and understanding.

Signature Dr. Charnetta

Date Today

Let's Be Intentional!

Now's the time to think about your desires for the month.
Reflect on the parenting prescription and write how it makes you feel.

Now, take a moment to jot down your deepest desires you'd like to achieve this month (e.g. - spend more time with my kids, feel better in my own skin, etc...). Reflect on them often.

THIS WEEK

Dates

3 Goals I'd Like To Achieve This Week:

1.

2.

3.

2 Things I Am Grateful For:

1.

2.

My Intention For This Week:

Mark the day(s) you achieved this intention. Write notes about how it feels to complete it.

M	T	W	T	F	S	S

I will validate my child's emotions, even if I don't fully understand them, to show that their feelings are heard and respected.

How do you initiate conversations with your tween/teen about sensitive topics, such as mental health, relationships, or school challenges? How can you create a safe space for them to open up?

COMMUNICATION BUILDER

Empathy Exercises: Put yourself in your teen's shoes to better understand their feelings and challenges.

THIS WEEK

Dates

3 Goals I'd Like To Achieve This Week:

1

2

3

2 Things I Am Grateful For:

1

2

My Intention For This Week:

Mark the day(s) you achieved this intention. Write notes about how it feels to complete it.

M	T	W	T	F	S	S

I intend to involve my tween/teen in family decisions, making them feel valued and included in important matters.

Write about a time when you and your tween/teen faced a conflict. How did you resolve it, and what communication techniques could improve future discussions?

"When your teen feels seen and heard, they'll open their eyes to your guidance."

THIS WEEK

Dates

3 Goals I'd Like To Achieve This Week:

1

2

3

2 Things I Am Grateful For:

1

2

My Intention For This Week:

Mark the day(s) you achieved this intention. Write notes about how it feels to complete it.

M	T	W	T	F	S	S

My focus will be on engaging in mindful conversations, giving my full attention and avoiding distractions, especially my cell phone.

Explore any changes you've noticed in your tween/teen's behavior or interests. How can you adapt and connect with them during this phase?

STRESS BUSTER

Practice Self-Care: Prioritize self-care to recharge and maintain emotional well-being, allowing you to better support your tween/teen.

THIS WEEK

____
Dates

3 Goals I'd Like To Achieve This Week:

1.

2.

3.

2 Things I Am Grateful For:

1.

2.

My Intention For This Week:

Mark the day(s) you achieved this intention. Write notes about how it feels to complete it.

M	T	W	T	F	S	S

I will express gratitude and appreciation to my tween/teen for their efforts and contributions.

Reflect on the most important life lessons you want to teach your tween/teen. How can you incorporate these lessons into your everyday interactions?

Bond Booster

Cooking Together: Prepare a meal or bake some treats together, enjoying quality time and creating lasting memories in the kitchen.

Rx

PARENT PRESCRIPTION

Directions:

Dear Parent,

Let go of perfection and embrace the imperfections of parenting, knowing that love is what truly matters.

Signature Dr. Charnetta

Date Today

Let's Be Intentional!

Now's the time to think about your desires for the month.
Reflect on the parenting prescription and write how it makes you feel.

Now, take a moment to jot down your deepest desires you'd like to achieve this month (e.g. - spend more time with my kids, feel better in my own skin, etc...). Reflect on them often.

THIS WEEK

____
Dates

3 Goals I'd Like To Achieve This Week:

1.

2.

3.

2 Things I Am Grateful For:

1.

2.

My Intention For This Week:

Mark the day(s) you achieved this intention. Write notes about how it feels to complete it.

M	T	W	T	F	S	S

I will model apologizing when I'm wrong and forgiving when necessary, promoting humility and empathy.

Think back to your own teenage years. How do those memories shape the way you're navigating the parenting journey with your tween or teen?

COMMUNICATION BUILDER

Reflective Responses: Mirror your child's emotions back to show that you understand and validate their feelings.

THIS WEEK

Dates

3 Goals I'd Like To Achieve This Week:

1.

2.

3.

2 Things I Am Grateful For:

1.

2.

My Intention For This Week:

Mark the day(s) you achieved this intention. Write notes about how it feels to complete it.

M	T	W	T	F	S	S

My goal is to share stories and anecdotes from my past, creating a sense of connection and understanding.

Explore your relationship with your tween/teen's other parent or co-parent. What strengths can you build upon, and how can you communicate more effectively as a parenting team?

“Parenting tweens/teens can be challenging, but the small victories are worth celebrating.”

THIS WEEK

Dates

3 Goals I'd Like To Achieve This Week:

1

2

3

2 Things I Am Grateful For:

1

2

My Intention For This Week:

Mark the day(s) you achieved this intention. Write notes about how it feels to complete it.

M	T	W	T	F	S	S

I will clearly communicate and establish boundaries that respect both my needs and my tween/teen's independence.

Write about a disagreement you had with your tween/teen. How did it impact your relationship, and what steps can you take to rebuild trust and understanding?

STRESS BUSTER

Laugh Together: Infuse humor into your interactions with your tween/teen, creating a positive atmosphere even during stressful times.

THIS WEEK

Dates

3 Goals I'd Like To Achieve This Week:

1.

2.

3.

2 Things I Am Grateful For:

1.

2.

My Intention For This Week:

Mark the day(s) you achieved this intention. Write notes about how it feels to complete it.

M	T	W	T	F	S	S

I intend to explore my child's interests and hobbies, seeking opportunities for shared experiences.

Write about a time when you felt overwhelmed by societal expectations of parenting. How can you stay true to your values and focus on your tween/teen's individual needs?

Bond Booster

Movie Marathon: Have a movie night with your tween/teen, complete with popcorn. Take turns picking films and discussing your favorite parts afterward.

Rx

Parent Prescription

Directions:

Dear Parent,

Getting your tween/teen to talk can feel like mission impossible. Nurture open conversations with your tween/teen, so they feel comfy sharing their thoughts and feelings with you.

Signature Dr. Charnetta

Date Today

Let's Be Intentional!

Now's the time to think about your desires for the month. Reflect on the parenting prescription and write how it makes you feel.

Now, take a moment to jot down your deepest desires you'd like to achieve this month (e.g. - spend more time with my kids, feel better in my own skin, etc...). Reflect on them often.

THIS WEEK

Dates

3 Goals I'd Like To Achieve This Week:

1

2

3

2 Things I Am Grateful For:

1

2

My Intention For This Week:

Mark the day(s) you achieved this intention. Write notes about how it feels to complete it.

M	T	W	T	F	S	S

This week, I aim to acknowledge my child's growth and development, highlighting their progress and achievements.

Reflect on a time when you felt you didn't understand your tween/teen's perspective. How can you bridge the generation gap and encourage open communication?

COMMUNICATION BUILDER

Open-Ended Questions: Use questions that encourage thoughtful responses and deeper conversations.

THIS WEEK

Dates

3 Goals I'd Like To Achieve This Week:

1

2

3

2 Things I Am Grateful For:

1

2

My Intention For This Week:

Mark the day(s) you achieved this intention. Write notes about how it feels to complete it.

M	T	W	T	F	S	S

I will exchange positive affirmations with my tween/teen, building their self-esteem and nurturing a positive relationship.

Write about a memorable family experience that brought you closer to your tween/teen. How can you create more opportunities for shared experiences?

"Believe in your tween/teen even when they doubt themselves because your faith will ignite their inner strength."

THIS WEEK

Dates

3 Goals I'd Like To Achieve This Week:

1

2

3

2 Things I Am Grateful For:

1

2

My Intention For This Week:

Mark the day(s) you achieved this intention. Write notes about how it feels to complete it.

M	T	W	T	F	S	S

My intention is to approach conversations with an open mind, respecting my child's opinions and encouraging dialogue.

Describe your favorite activity to do with your tween/teen. How does this activity enhance your bond, and how can you incorporate more quality time into your routine?

STRESS BUSTER

Take Breaks: Step away from challenging situations when needed, giving yourself time to regain composure and perspective.

THIS WEEK

Dates

3 Goals I'd Like To Achieve This Week:

1

2

3

2 Things I Am Grateful For:

1

2

My Intention For This Week:

Mark the day(s) you achieved this intention. Write notes about how it feels to complete it.

M	T	W	T	F	S	S

I will set aside time to ask my tween/teen thought-provoking questions, nudging us into deeper conversations.

List 3 of your favorite qualities and personality traits in your tween/teen. How can you celebrate and nurture these unique characteristics?

Bond Booster

Outdoor Adventure: Go for a hike, bike ride, or simply spend time in nature, connecting while exploring the great outdoors.

Rx

Parent Prescription

Directions:

Dear Parent,

Release the need to control every outcome and trust in your child's ability to make positive choices.

Signature Dr. Charnetta

Date Today

Let's Be Intentional!

Now's the time to think about your desires for the month.
Reflect on the parenting prescription and write how it makes you feel.

Now, take a moment to jot down your deepest desires you'd like to achieve this month (e.g. - spend more time with my kids, feel better in my own skin, etc...). Reflect on them often.

THIS WEEK

Dates

3 Goals I'd Like To Achieve This Week:

1.

2.

3.

2 Things I Am Grateful For:

1.

2.

My Intention For This Week:

Mark the day(s) you achieved this intention. Write notes about how it feels to complete it.

M	T	W	T	F	S	S

This week, I intend to maintain a calm and composed presence, even during challenging conversations.

Describe a moment when you felt proud of your tween/teen's growth and maturity. How can you encourage and support further development?

COMMUNICATION BUILDER

Patience and Pause: Take a moment before responding during heated discussions to avoid escalating conflicts.

THIS WEEK

Dates

3 Goals I'd Like To Achieve This Week:

1

2

3

2 Things I Am Grateful For:

1

2

My Intention For This Week:

Mark the day(s) you achieved this intention. Write notes about how it feels to complete it.

M T W T F S S

I will celebrate my tween/teen's individuality and interests, supporting them in being their authentic selves.

Write about a cherished memory from your tween/teen's childhood. How does this memory impact your parenting approach today?

"Be the soft place for your tween/teen to land in difficult times so that they know you'll always be there to guide them."

THIS WEEK

Dates

3 Goals I'd Like To Achieve This Week:

1

2

3

2 Things I Am Grateful For:

1

2

My Intention For This Week:

Mark the day(s) you achieved this intention. Write notes about how it feels to complete it.

M	T	W	T	F	S	S

My intention is to express gratitude regularly, focusing on the positives in our relationship and interactions.

Write about a challenge you faced while balancing work and parenting responsibilities. How can you create a healthier work-life balance?

STRESS BUSTER

Connect with Other Parents: Join parent support groups or online communities to share experiences, tips, and find comfort in knowing you're not alone.

THIS WEEK

Dates

3 Goals I'd Like To Achieve This Week:

1

2

3

2 Things I Am Grateful For:

1

2

My Intention For This Week:

Mark the day(s) you achieved this intention. Write notes about how it feels to complete it.

M T W T F S S

I will ask open-ended questions that encourage deeper thinking and conversations with my tween/teen.

Explore any fears or concerns you have about your tween/teen's future. How can you turn these worries into proactive actions?

Bond Booster

Arts and Crafts: Engage in a creative session, whether it's painting, craft ng, or DIY projects, to bond through artistic expression.

Rx

Parent Prescription

Directions:

Dear Parent,

Don't be so hard on your child and don't be so hard on yourself. Sometimes the pressure can be too much for both of you.

Signature Dr. Charnetta

Date Today

Let's Be Intentional!

Now's the time to think about your desires for the month.
Reflect on the parenting prescription and write how it makes you feel.

Now, take a moment to jot down your deepest desires you'd like to achieve this month (e.g. - spend more time with my kids, feel better in my own skin, etc...). Reflect on them often.

THIS WEEK

Dates

3 Goals I'd Like To Achieve This Week:

1.

2.

3.

2 Things I Am Grateful For:

1.

2.

My Intention For This Week:

Mark the day(s) you achieved this intention. Write notes about how it feels to complete it.

M T W T F S S

My intention is to reflect on the progress we've made in our communication and relationship, celebrating the milestones we've achieved.

Reflect on a recent interaction with your tween/teen that brought you joy. What made it special, and how can you recreate such moments?

COMMUNICATION BUILDER

Positive Reinforcement: Use praise and encouragement to motivate positive behavior and boost self-esteem.

THIS WEEK

____
Dates

3 Goals I'd Like To Achieve This Week:

1.

2.

3.

2 Things I Am Grateful For:

1.

2.

My Intention For This Week:

Mark the day(s) you achieved this intention. Write notes about how it feels to complete it.

M	T	W	T	F	S	S

This week, my intention is to put myself in my tween/teen's shoes and empathize with their perspective on various matters.

Explore any unmet expectations you have as a parent. How can you redefine these expectations to cultivate a more positive parenting experience?

"In moments of doubt, remember the powerful influence you have over your tween/teens life."

THIS WEEK

Dates

3 Goals I'd Like To Achieve This Week:

1.

2.

3.

2 Things I Am Grateful For:

1.

2.

My Intention For This Week:

Mark the day(s) you achieved this intention. Write notes about how it feels to complete it.

M	T	W	T	F	S	S

I intend to prioritize shared meals without distractions, creating a space for meaningful conversations and connection.

Reflect on the importance of self-care and its impact on your parenting. How can you prioritize self-care to be a more present and patient parent?

STRESS BUSTER

Have a "Role Reversal Day" where your teen takes on some of your responsibilities and you take on theirs. This fun and enlightening experience can build empathy and understanding between you as well as alleviate some of your stress.

THIS WEEK

Dates

3 Goals I'd Like To Achieve This Week:

1

2

3

2 Things I Am Grateful For:

1

2

My Intention For This Week:

Mark the day(s) you achieved this intention. Write notes about how it feels to complete it.

M	T	W	T	F	S	S

My goal is to support my tween/teen in making decisions and taking responsibility, empowering them to grow independently.

Explore your parenting goals for the future. What steps can you take to align your actions with these aspirations?

Bond Booster

Reading Club: Start a book club between you and your tween/teen, discussing your favorite reads and sharing your thoughts.

Rx

Parent Prescription

Directions:

Dear Parent,

Every step you take, every conversation you have, brings you closer to your tween/teen. Your presence is shaping their world in beautiful ways.

Signature Dr. Charnetta

Date Today

Let's Be Intentional!

Now's the time to think about your desires for the month.
Reflect on the parenting prescription and write how it makes you feel.

Now, take a moment to jot down your deepest desires you'd like to achieve this month (e.g. - spend more time with my kids, feel better in my own skin, etc...). Reflect on them often.

THIS WEEK

Dates

3 Goals I'd Like To Achieve This Week:

1.

2.

3.

2 Things I Am Grateful For:

1.

2.

My Intention For This Week:

Mark the day(s) you achieved this intention. Write notes about how it feels to complete it.

M	T	W	T	F	S	S

I will practice being fully present during our interactions, minimizing distractions and showing my complete attention.

Write about a challenge your tween/teen is currently facing. How can you offer guidance and support without being overbearing?

COMMUNICATION BUILDER

I-Statements: Share your feelings using "I feel" statements to avoid sounding accusatory.

THIS WEEK

Dates

3 Goals I'd Like To Achieve This Week:

1.

2.

3.

2 Things I Am Grateful For:

1.

2.

My Intention For This Week:

Mark the day(s) you achieved this intention. Write notes about how it feels to complete it.

M T W T F S S

This week, I intend to encourage my tween/teen to keep a journal and share our thoughts and reflections with each other.

Reflect on a time when you were vulnerable with your tween/teen. How did it impact your relationship, and how can you continue to be open and authentic with them?

"Parenting a tween/teen is discovering new layers of love and resilience you never knew you had."

THIS WEEK

Dates

3 Goals I'd Like To Achieve This Week:

1.

2.

3.

2 Things I Am Grateful For:

1.

2.

My Intention For This Week:

Mark the day(s) you achieved this intention. Write notes about how it feels to complete it.

M	T	W	T	F	S	S

I will explore and understand my tween/teen's love language, tailoring my actions to make them feel loved and valued.

What are the common stress triggers you experience while parenting your tween/teen? How can you manage or minimize them?

STRESS BUSTER

Plan a spa day at home with your teen, complete with facials, DIY treatments, and relaxation exercises. This shared self-care experience can create deeper connections and relaxation for both of you.

THIS WEEK

____
Dates

3 Goals I'd Like To Achieve This Week:

1.

2.

3.

2 Things I Am Grateful For:

1.

2.

My Intention For This Week:

Mark the day(s) you achieved this intention. Write notes about how it feels to complete it.

M	T	W	T	F	S	S

I will explore my tween/teen's interests with genuine curiosity, showing enthusiasm for their passions.

Describe a situation where you had different expectations for your child's choices. How can you find a balance between guiding them and respecting their autonomy?

Bond Booster

Volunteer Together: Find a local charity or community service activity to contribute to together, instilling the value of giving back.

Rx

PARENT PRESCRIPTION

Directions:

Dear Parent,

Trust your instincts as a parent and make decisions with confidence.

Signature Dr. Charnetta

Date Today

Let's Be Intentional!

Now's the time to think about your desires for the month.
Reflect on the parenting prescription and write how it makes you feel.

Now, take a moment to jot down your deepest desires you'd like to achieve this month (e.g. - spend more time with my kids, feel better in my own skin, etc...). Reflect on them often.

THIS WEEK

Dates

3 Goals I'd Like To Achieve This Week:

1.

2.

3.

2 Things I Am Grateful For:

1.

2.

My Intention For This Week:

Mark the day(s) you achieved this intention. Write notes about how it feels to complete it.

M	T	W	T	F	S	S

I intend to set aside dedicated time for heart-to-heart talks where we can discuss deeper matters.

Write about a time when you and your tween/teen bonded over a shared interest or hobby. How can you explore more activities together to enhance your relationship?

COMMUNICATION BUILDER

Setting Boundaries: Communicate clear expectations and boundaries while maintaining a supportive environment.

THIS WEEK

Dates

3 Goals I'd Like To Achieve This Week:

1

2

3

2 Things I Am Grateful For:

1

2

My Intention For This Week:

Mark the day(s) you achieved this intention. Write notes about how it feels to complete it.

M	T	W	T	F	S	S

This week, I aim to provide consistent positive reinforcement for their efforts and accomplishments.

How do you model healthy coping mechanisms and emotional regulation for your child? How can you improve your own responses to stress and emotions?

"Embrace the imperfections of parenting, for it is through mistakes that we learn, grow, and become better guides for our children."

THIS WEEK

Dates

3 Goals I'd Like To Achieve This Week:

1

2

3

2 Things I Am Grateful For:

1

2

My Intention For This Week:

Mark the day(s) you achieved this intention. Write notes about how it feels to complete it.

M	T	W	T	F	S	S

My goal is to practice patience during moments of disagreement or frustration, allowing for more constructive conversations.

What are some positive changes you've noticed in your tween/teen recently? How can you express your pride and encouragement for their growth?

STRESS BUSTER

Practice Mindfulness: Engage in mindfulness techniques to stay present and avoid unnecessary worry about the past or future.

THIS WEEK

Dates

3 Goals I'd Like To Achieve This Week:

1

2

3

2 Things I Am Grateful For:

1

2

My Intention For This Week:

Mark the day(s) you achieved this intention. Write notes about how it feels to complete it.

M	T	W	T	F	S	S

I will encourage us to have designated time away from screens, promoting face-to-face interactions.

Reflect on your own experiences of being misunderstood as a teenager. How does this reflection shape the way you listen to and validate your child's feelings?

Bond Booster

Sports or Exercise: Participate in physical activities like playing a sport, going for a run, or practicing yoga together.

℞

Parent Prescription

Directions:

Dear Parent,

It's okay to feel uncertain at times. your commitment to learning and growing alongside your tween/teen is what truly matters.

Signature Dr. Charnetta

Date Today

Let's Be Intentional!

**Now's the time to think about your desires for the month.
Reflect on the parenting prescription and write how it makes you feel.**

Now, take a moment to jot down your deepest desires you'd like to achieve this month (e.g. - spend more time with my kids, feel better in my own skin, etc...). Reflect on them often.

THIS WEEK

Dates

3 Goals I'd Like To Achieve This Week:

1

2

3

2 Things I Am Grateful For:

1

2

My Intention For This Week:

Mark the day(s) you achieved this intention. Write notes about how it feels to complete it.

M	T	W	T	F	S	S

This week, I intend to encourage my tween/teen to share their dreams and goals, offering guidance and support.

Reflect on a time when you felt disconnected from your tween/teen. How can you create opportunities to reconnect and strengthen your relationship?

COMMUNICATION BUILDER

Tech-Free Time: Set aside regular tech-free moments to connect and engage in face-to-face conversations.

THIS WEEK

Dates

3 Goals I'd Like To Achieve This Week:

1

2

3

2 Things I Am Grateful For:

1

2

My Intention For This Week:

Mark the day(s) you achieved this intention. Write notes about how it feels to complete it.

M T W T F S S

I intend to create a problem-free zone during meals or specific times where we focus on positive discussions.

Reflect on a time when you had to let go of control and allow your tween/teen to make their own decisions. How did you handle it, and what can you do to promote independence responsibly?

"Communication is the bridge that connects hearts and minds. Keep the conversation flowing, and the bond will flourish."

THIS WEEK

Dates

3 Goals I'd Like To Achieve This Week:

1

2

3

2 Things I Am Grateful For:

1

2

My Intention For This Week:

Mark the day(s) you achieved this intention. Write notes about how it feels to complete it.

M	T	W	T	F	S	S

My intention is to reflect on the positives in our relationship and express gratitude for the role my tween/teen plays in my life.

What are some barriers to open communication with your tween/teen? How can you overcome these barriers and foster better communication?

STRESS BUSTER

Limit Technology Use: Constant connectivity can add to stress. Take breaks from screens, especially before bed, to give your mind a chance to relax.

THIS WEEK

Dates

3 Goals I'd Like To Achieve This Week:

1

2

3

2 Things I Am Grateful For:

1

2

My Intention For This Week:

Mark the day(s) you achieved this intention. Write notes about how it feels to complete it.

M	T	W	T	F	S	S

My goal is to discuss and reflect on our family values, ensuring they guide our interactions and decisions.

How can you empower your tween/teen to make informed decisions in the face of peer pressure? How can you encourage open dialogue about friendships and relationships?

Bond Booster

Cook-Off Challenge: Have a cooking competition where each family member creates a dish, and everyone tastes and rates the results.

Rx PARENT PRESCRIPTION

Directions:

Dear Parent,

Through the ups and downs, your unwavering dedication is shaping your child's journey into adulthood. Don't give up.

Signature Dr. Charnetta

Date Today

Let's Be Intentional!

Now's the time to think about your desires for the month.
Reflect on the parenting prescription and write how it makes you feel.

Now, take a moment to jot down your deepest desires you'd like to achieve this month (e.g. - spend more time with my kids, feel better in my own skin, etc...). Reflect on them often.

THIS WEEK

____
Dates

3 Goals I'd Like To Achieve This Week:

1

2

3

2 Things I Am Grateful For:

1

2

My Intention For This Week:

Mark the day(s) you achieved this intention. Write notes about how it feels to complete it.

M	T	W	T	F	S	S

My intention is to provide constructive feedback in a mindful and gentle manner, promoting growth and learning.

How do you set boundaries with your tween/teen while keeping lines of communication open? How can you reinforce the idea that they can trust you with their concerns?

COMMUNICATION BUILDER

Family Meetings: Schedule regular family meetings to discuss important topics and make collective decisions.

THIS WEEK

Dates

3 Goals I'd Like To Achieve This Week:

1.

2.

3.

2 Things I Am Grateful For:

1.

2.

My Intention For This Week:

Mark the day(s) you achieved this intention. Write notes about how it feels to complete it.

M	T	W	T	F	S	S

My intention is to engage in creative forms of communication, such as writing letters or creating art together.

What are three things you are grateful for about your tween/teen? How can you express this gratitude to reinforce the positive aspects of your relationship?

"In the whirlwind of parenting, find balance by staying present in each moment, cherishing the joy, and facing the challenges with resilience."

THIS WEEK

Dates

3 Goals I'd Like To Achieve This Week:

1

2

3

2 Things I Am Grateful For:

1

2

My Intention For This Week:

Mark the day(s) you achieved this intention. Write notes about how it feels to complete it.

M	T	W	T	F	S	S

I will prioritize building and maintaining trust with my tween/teen, ensuring they feel comfortable sharing their thoughts.

How do you handle emotional ups and downs in your tween/teen during puberty? What strategies do you use to support them through these changes?

STRESS BUSTER

Seek Professional Help: If stress becomes overwhelming or persistent, consider speaking to a mental health professional. Therapy, counseling, or stress management workshops can provide effective strategies tailored to your needs.

THIS WEEK

Dates

3 Goals I'd Like To Achieve This Week:

1.

2.

3.

2 Things I Am Grateful For:

1.

2.

My Intention For This Week:

Mark the day(s) you achieved this intention. Write notes about how it feels to complete it.

M	T	W	T	F	S	S

This week, I aim to engage in activities we've never tried before, sparking fresh conversations and experiences.

Reflect on your own communication style and patterns. How can you model open communication for your child and encourage them to share openly with you?

Bond Booster

Day Trip Adventure: Plan a day trip to a nearby town or attraction, exploring new places and enjoying a change of scenery.

Rx

Parent Prescription

Directions:

Dear Parent,

With your encouragement and understanding, your tween/teen can learn to use their cell phone responsibly while still enjoying a well-rounded life.

Signature Dr. Charnetta

Date Today

Let's Be Intentional!

Now's the time to think about your desires for the month.
Reflect on the parenting prescription and write how it makes you feel.

Now, take a moment to jot down your deepest desires you'd like to achieve this month (e.g. - spend more time with my kids, feel better in my own skin, etc...). Reflect on them often.

THIS WEEK

Dates

3 Goals I'd Like To Achieve This Week:

1

2

3

2 Things I Am Grateful For:

1

2

My Intention For This Week:

Mark the day(s) you achieved this intention. Write notes about how it feels to complete it.

M	T	W	T	F	S	S

My goal is to allow room for spontaneous conversations to arise naturally, without forcing any specific topic.

How can you create an open and non-judgmental space for your child to express their emotions during moments of emotional turbulence?

COMMUNICATION BUILDER

Appreciation Notes: Write small notes of appreciation to show your love and gratitude to your tween/teen.

THIS WEEK

Dates

3 Goals I'd Like To Achieve This Week:

1

2

3

2 Things I Am Grateful For:

1

2

My Intention For This Week:

Mark the day(s) you achieved this intention. Write notes about how it feels to complete it.

M	T	W	T	F	S	S

This week, I intend to explore cultural activities or events together, broadening our perspectives and discussions.

Write a letter to your younger self, offering advice and insights about raising tweens and teens.

"Your belief in your tween/teen's potential will fuel their self-confidence to achieve greatness."

THIS WEEK

Dates

3 Goals I'd Like To Achieve This Week:

1

2

3

2 Things I Am Grateful For:

1

2

My Intention For This Week:

Mark the day(s) you achieved this intention. Write notes about how it feels to complete it.

M T W T F S S

I will establish positive morning routines that include meaningful interactions to start our days on a positive note.

List three emotional changes you've noticed in your tween/teen during puberty. How can you communicate your awareness and acceptance of these changes?

STRESS BUSTER

Engage in Hobbies: Pursuing activities you enjoy can divert your mind from stressors and provide a sense of accomplishment. Whether it's painting, playing an instrument, or gardening, hobbies can be therapeutic.

THIS WEEK

____
Dates

3 Goals I'd Like To Achieve This Week:

1

2

3

2 Things I Am Grateful For:

1

2

My Intention For This Week:

Mark the day(s) you achieved this intention. Write notes about how it feels to complete it.

M	T	W	T	F	S	S

This week, I intend to have conversations about media, discussing movies, books, or news to exchange viewpoints.

Describe a topic you've been hesitant to discuss with your tween/teen. How can you approach this conversation with curiosity and openness, promoting trust and comfort?

Bond Booster

Memory Lane Journey: Look through old photo albums or home videos, reminiscing about precious family memories.

Rx

PARENT PRESCRIPTION

Directions:

Dear Parent,

Express gratitude for the gift of parenting and cherish every moment of this incredible journey.

Signature Dr. Charnetta

Date Today

Let's Be Intentional!

Now's the time to think about your desires for the month.
Reflect on the parenting prescription and write how it makes you feel.

Now, take a moment to jot down your deepest desires you'd like to achieve this month (e.g. - spend more time with my kids, feel better in my own skin, etc...). Reflect on them often.

THIS WEEK

Dates

3 Goals I'd Like To Achieve This Week:

1

2

3

2 Things I Am Grateful For:

1

2

My Intention For This Week:

Mark the day(s) you achieved this intention. Write notes about how it feels to complete it.

M	T	W	T	F	S	S

I will encourage my tween/teen to set personal goals and support them in achieving these aspirations.

Describe your proudest moment as a parent to your tween/teen. What made this moment stand out, and how did it impact your relationship?

COMMUNICATION BUILDER

Open and Non-Judgmental Attitude: Create an environment where your teen feels comfortable expressing themselves without fear of judgment. Avoid criticizing or lecturing.

THIS WEEK

Dates

3 Goals I'd Like To Achieve This Week:

1.

2.

3.

2 Things I Am Grateful For:

1.

2.

My Intention For This Week:

Mark the day(s) you achieved this intention. Write notes about how it feels to complete it.

M	T	W	T	F	S	S

My goal is to involve my tween/teen in collaborative problem-solving, encouraging them to contribute ideas and solutions.

Describe a time when your tween/teen surprised you with their resilience and strength. How can you continue to encourage their self-confidence?

"Every moment spent with your tween or teen is a chance to make memories and build a lifetime of love."

THIS WEEK

Dates

3 Goals I'd Like To Achieve This Week:

1

2

3

2 Things I Am Grateful For:

1

2

My Intention For This Week:

Mark the day(s) you achieved this intention. Write notes about how it feels to complete it.

M	T	W	T	F	S	S

This week, I aim to learn about my tween/teen's interests, music, and pop culture, creating shared experiences.

Describe a recent situation where you empathized with your tween/teen's emotions. How did your empathy impact the way you responded to their feelings?

STRESS BUSTER

Get Adequate Sleep: Prioritize quality sleep by establishing a consistent sleep schedule and creating a calming bedtime routine. A well-rested body is better equipped to handle stress.

THIS WEEK

Dates

3 Goals I'd Like To Achieve This Week:

1

2

3

2 Things I Am Grateful For:

1

2

My Intention For This Week:

Mark the day(s) you cchieved this intention. Write notes about how it feels to complete it.

M	T	W	T	F	S	S

I intend to address any lingering conflicts, practicing forgiveness and letting go of negative emotions.

Reflect on where you started when you began this journal and where you are now as far as the relationship with your tween/teen.

Bond Booster

Stargazing Night: Spend an evening under the stars, either in your backyard or at a local observatory, discussing the wonders of the universe.

NOTE TO SELF

NOTE TO SELF

NOTE TO SELF

NOTE TO SELF

MEET DR. CHARNETTA

Dr. Charnetta Coltor-Poole (a.k.a. Dr. CeCe) is a Board-certified Pediatrician, tween and teen whole health expert and communication strategist, speaker, and writer. A true Georgia peach, Dr. Charnetta received her Bachelor of Science degree from the University of Georgia and her Master of Science degree from Georgia State University. She received her Doctor of Medicine degree from Morehouse School of Medicine and completed her Pediatric and Adolescent Medicine Residency at Emory University School of Medicine in Atlanta, GA. Dr. Charnetta has over 25 years experience in the writing field and is the Amazon #1 Best-Selling Author of 'The 10 Commandments of Communication for Doctors,' and Write Through It Journal: A Guided Journal For Teen Girls. She is also a Christian playwright with multiple writing and directing credits to her name. Dr. Charnetta is a recipient of the University of Georgia Top 40 under 40 Alumni award, the Billie Wright Adams Excellence in Medicine award, and Georgia Trend Magazine 2020 Top Doc Award. She is also an active member of Alpha Kappa Alpha Sorority, Inc. She is a proud wife and mom and enjoys spending time with family, singing, and SEC Football. She is passionate about helping parents raise confident, empathetic, and mentally and physically healthy tweens and teens.

Made in the USA
Columbia, SC
25 November 2023

27108426R00100